Table of Contents

....	1
Introduction	3
Patsas Soup	4
Chicken and Quinoa Greek Salad	6
Greek Beans and Seared Lamb	8
Fakes	10
Greek Skinos	12
Tomato Spread Dip invent	14
Tapenade Skordalia	16
Amba Sauce	18
Yogurt Sauce	20
Greek Salad Omelet	21
Ouzotini	23
Shrimps a la Spetsiota	25
Greek Ravani	27
Kakavia	29
Feta, Chili oil, and Thyme	31
Poor Man's Caviar	33
Greek Mimosa	35
Sex on the Greek!!	37
Ambrosia Drink	39
Honey, Walnuts, and Yogurt	41
Tzatziki	43
Spicy Watermelon Salad	45
Avgolemono	47
Greek Mojito	49
Greek Chocolate Mousse and Biscuits	51
Greek Salad	53
Greek Doctor	55
Galotyri	57
Chickpea Soup	59
Fasolatha	61
Conclusion	63

The Undefeatable Greek Recipes
Classical Greek Meals Fit for Gods And Goddesses

BY: Ida Smith
Copyright © 2021 by Ida Smith. All Rights Reserved.

License Notes

This book is licensed for your personal enjoyment only. This book may not be re-sold or given away to other people. If you would like to share this book with another person, please purchase an additional copy for each recipient. If you're reading this book and did not purchase it, or it was not purchased for your use only, then please return to your favorite ebook retailer and purchase your own copy. Thank you for respecting the hard work of this author.

Introduction

We all know that it is not every day that you come in contact with meals that are deserving of gods and goddesses. This is why we have created this Greek Cookbook for your godly exploration, for you to have a delicious feeling of what the gods and goddesses of Greek feed on.

Do you want to cook, dine, and feast like a Greek god and goddess, then this is the cookbook that you need to have right there with you!!

Patsas Soup

If you are a pork lover, this recipe is for you!

Preparation Time: 10 minutes
Cooking time: 2 hours
Makes: 2
Ingredient list:

- 250g cubed pork belly
- 1 teaspoon salt
- 1 teaspoon pepper
- 1 lemon
- 250g chopped pork leg
- 1 sliced chili pepper

Preparation:
Put the pork belly and legs in a pot of water.
Cook for 13 minutes till it boils.
Discard the water.
Pour another water into the pot.
Cook the meat again for another 1 hour 30 minutes to soften it.
Add seasonings and lemon juice.
Boil for 15 minutes more.
Serve and enjoy.

Chicken and Quinoa Greek Salad

Vibrant and flavorful!!!
Preparation Time: 10 minutes
Cooking time: 25 minutes
Makes: 1
Ingredient list:

- 4 tablespoons cooked red quinoa
- 1 boneless chicken (skinless and dried)
- 1 oz feta cheese
- 1 minced garlic clove
- 1 handful pitted olives (chopped)
- 1 handful chopped sweet piquante pepper
- 1 teaspoon salt

- 1 teaspoon pepper
- 2 tablespoons olive oil
- 2 oz diced sweet peppers (cored and with stem removed)
- 1 teaspoon vinegar (apple cider)
- 1 sliced sweet onion
- 1 teaspoon dried oregano

Preparation:
Combine the garlic, salt, pepper, vinegar, oregano, and olive oil in a bowl. Whisk well to marinate.
Season the chicken and cook in a pan of oil.
Cook till the chicken is cooked and browned.
Transfer to a paper-lined plate and slice when it gets cool.
Pour oil in the pan, add the onion, sweet peppers, pepper, and salt.
Cook for 6 minutes.
Pour the cooked quinoa into a pot, add the pepper mixture, pepper, salt, olives, and piquante peppers.
Add a drizzle of the oregano mixture.
Mix well.
Serve with chicken and cheese.

Greek Beans and Seared Lamb

This dish is inspired by the virgin goddess, Artemis!!!

Preparation Time: 05 minutes
Cooking time: 15 minutes
Makes: 2
Ingredient list:

- 2 crushed garlic cloves
- 1 teaspoon pepper
- 1 teaspoon salt
- 250g lamb fillet (sliced)
- 1 handful chopped dill
- 400g drained butter beans
- 200ml chicken broth

- 1 tablespoon olive oil
- 1 chopped medium onion
- 1 teaspoon red wine vinegar
- 1 tablespoon tomato puree
- 1 tablespoon crushed feta cheese

Preparation:
Coat the lamb in one part of the garlic, pepper, salt, and a little oil.
Toss well and keep aside.
Pour the remaining oil into a pan, add in the remaining part of garlic, pepper, salt, and onions. Cook for 2 minutes.
Throw in the dill, broth, tomato puree, vinegar, and beans.
Cook for 11 minutes till most of the liquid has been absorbed.
Pour oil in another pan, sauté the lamb slices till done.
Serve the beans mixture with the lamb, and garnish with feta.

Fakes

No!!!! It is not "fakes" as in "fakes", but it is "fakes" as in "fakes".

Arrgh!! You know what? Ignore the name and just enjoy this delicious and flavorful Greek lentil soup that was once Zeus' favorite meal!!

Preparation Time: 30 minutes
Cooking time: 1 hour 40 minutes
Makes: 6
Ingredient list:

- 2 minced small-sized onions
- 12 ounces brown lentils
- 1 tablespoon oregano
- 8 tablespoons oil
- 2 quarts water

- 2 tablespoons garlic minced
- 2 small chopped carrot
- 3 bay leaves
- 1 teaspoon salt
- 1 tablespoon pepper
- 2 tablespoons tomato paste
- 1 teaspoon crushed rosemary (dried)

Preparation:
Pour the oil into a pan. Add the carrot, onion, and garlic.
Cook-stir for 8 minutes.
Add in the lentils, rosemary, oregano, bay leaves, and water.
Cook and allow simmering for 20 minutes.
Add in the salt, tomato paste, and pepper.
Cover and cover for another 55 minutes. Discard bay leaves.
Serve and enjoy.

Greek Skinos

Refreshing, just like the Hades god loves it!!!!

Preparation Time: 04 minutes
Cooking time: nil
Makes: 1
Ingredient list:

- 6 basil leaves
- 400ml Skinos
- 1 handful ice cubes
- 150ml soda water
- 150ml lemon juice
- 1 lemon wedge

Preparation:
Mix the first 5 ingredients in a mixer.
Mix well.
Strain into a glass.
Garnish with a lemon wedge.

Tomato Spread Dip invent

We know that you are not familiar with this recipe. Get familiar with this unique and sweet (yes, sweet) tomato delicacy that was invented by the goddess of beauty, Aphrodite!!!

Preparation Time: 10 minutes
Cooking time: 45 minutes
Makes: 2
Ingredient list:

- 1 tablespoon chopped mint
- 1 pound cored, seedless, skinless, fresh tomatoes (ripe)
- 1 tablespoons creta raki
- 1 cup feta cheese (mashed)
- 3 tablespoons Greek oil

Preparation:
Preheat your oven to 377 degrees F.
Brush oil all over a baking sheet, then place the tomatoes on the sheet.
Place sheet in the oven, and roast tomatoes for 45 minutes.
When they are shrunk, remove from oven and keep aside to cool.
Put the mashed cheese, remaining oil, creta raki, and tomatoes in a bowl.
Mash well.
Serve with a sprinkle of mint.

Tapenade Skordalia

Just a cool name for potato puree. This meal is one of the special creations of the Hephaestus!!

Preparation Time: 07 minutes
Cooking time: 15 minutes
Makes: 2
Ingredient list:

- 1 teaspoon green olive tapenade
- 70ml olive oil
- 1 minced garlic
- 400g chunked floury potatoes
- 1 teaspoon red wine vinegar

Preparation:

Boil the potatoes in a pot of water mixed with salt.
Drain the potatoes when they are tender.
Mash the potatoes in a bowl.
Throw in the olive oil, vinegar, tapenade, and garlic.
Mix well.

Amba Sauce

This delicious Amba sauce is made from mango for the goddess Demeter!!

Preparation Time: 05 minutes
Cooking time: 07 minutes
Makes: 2
Ingredient list:

- 4 tablespoons water
- 1 tablespoon olive oil
- 1 pinch fenugreek
- 1 minced garlic
- 1 pinch sumac
- 1 pinch cumin
- 1 teaspoon cayenne
- 1 diced fresh, ripe mango

- 1 pinch salt
- 1 teaspoon Dijon mustard
- 4 tablespoons lemon juice
- 3 tablespoons apple cider vinegar

Preparation:
Pour the oil into a pan.
Throw in the garlic. Cook-stir for 2 minutes.
Add the spices and mango.
Stir-fry for 2 minutes.
Add in the water, lemon, and vinegar.
Cook-stir for 4 minutes.
Blend when the mixture is cool.

Yogurt Sauce

Yogurt sauce???!!! You can't believe it!!

Preparation Time: 04 minutes
Cooking time: nil
Makes: 2
Ingredient list:

- 1 pinch salt
- 4 ounces cold yogurt
- 1 teaspoon lemon juice
- 1 minced garlic clove

Preparation:
Mix all ingredient in a bowl.

Greek Salad Omelet

This salad is perfect for a quick dinner on a work night!!!

Preparation Time: 05 minutes
Cooking time: 15 minutes
Makes: 3
Ingredient list:

- 70g crumbled feta cheese
- 1 tablespoon olive oil
- 6 eggs
- 1 handful chopped cilantro
- 1 tablespoon pepper
- 1 tablespoon salt
- 2 chopped tomatoes

- 1 chopped medium red onion
- 1 handful pitted black olives

Preparation:
Preheat the grill to 403 degrees F.
Whisk the eggs, cilantro, salt, and pepper in a bowl.
Pour the oil into a pan. Add in the onion.
Cook for 3 minutes. Add in the olives and tomatoes.
Cook for 2 minutes.
Add in the egg mixture. Cook for 2 minutes till they are half cooked but runny.
Add a sprinkle of feta.
Transfer the pan under your heated grill.
Cook for 4 minutes.
Serve and enjoy.

Ouzotini

This is much more than a cocktail; it is an ointment to be used for flu and winter ailments, just like Asclepius, the god of medicine.

Preparation Time: 04 minutes
Cooking time: nil
Makes: 1
Ingredient list:

- 1 teaspoon sugar
- 4 tablespoons pineapple juice
- 2 tablespoons vodka
- 2 tablespoons ouzo
- 1 handful ice cubes
- 1 dash lemon juice

Preparation:
Combine the second to the last ingredient in a shaker.
Shake well.
Rim the glass with sugar.
Strain the mixture into the glass.

Shrimps a la Spetsiota

This shrimp recipe is definitely fit for a beautiful goddess like Aphrodite!!!!!

Preparation Time: 05 minutes
Cooking time: 10 minutes
Makes: 4
Ingredient list:

- 2 grated large tomatoes
- 1 tablespoon olive oil
- 1 tablespoon salt
- 1 sliced medium onion
- 1 tablespoon white pepper
- 1 tablespoon Greek dried oregano
- 1 glass dry white wine

- 100g crumbled feta
- 400g large raw prawns (shrimps)
- 1 tablespoon chopped parsley

Preparation:
Pour the oil into a pan, then add in the onion.
Cook-fry for 2 minutes.
Add in the tomatoes.
Cook for 3 minutes before pouring in the white wine.
Add the salt, oregano, and pepper.
Cook for 3 minutes, and throw in the prawns.
Cook until they are down before adding the feta.
When the feta has melted, add the parsley.
Serve with bread.

Greek Ravani

This Greek coconut cake is perfect for everyone!!
Preparation Time: 20 minutes
Cooking time: 1 hour
Makes: 5 portions
Ingredient list:

- 2 cups lemon syrup
- 1 orange zest
- 4 tablespoons flour
- 1 cup flaked coconut
- 4 tablespoons butter
- 1 egg (separate the yolk and white)
- 6 tablespoons sugar
- 1 pinch baking powder

Preparation:
Preheat the oven to 354 degrees F.
Beat the egg white and a little bit of sugar to become meringue.
Whisk the sugar, yolk, and butter until fluffy.
Mix the baking powder, flour, and coconut in another bowl.
Add the meringue, the coconut mixture, and zest into the butter mixture.
Whisk well.
Butter the sides and bottom of your cake tin.
Add a sprinkle of flour.
Get rid of the excess flour in the tin.
Transfer the mixture into the tin.
Bake the cake till it is golden.
Serve the cake when it is cool, and garnish with a drop of the lemon syrup.

Kakavia

The name Kakavia didn't originally belong to this delicacy itself, but to the pot that the fishermen used to cook this delicacy and sacrifice to the god of the sea, Poseidon.

Enough of the history, let's make us some fisherman soup!!!

Preparation Time: 10 minutes
Cooking time: 30 minutes
Makes: 3
Ingredient list:

- 4 cups water
- 1 grated garlic clove
- 1 tablespoon chopped parsley
- 1 pound scaled, cleaned codfish
- 1 handful cleaned shrimps

- 1 diced celery stalk
- 1 diced and peeled potatoes
- 1 chopped onion
- 2 tablespoons olive oil
- 1 tablespoon salt
- 1 tablespoon pepper
- 7 ounces pureed tomatoes

Preparation:
Boil the fish in a pot of water.
Drain the fish but keep the fish broth.
Put the fish on a plate and remove the skin and bones.
Dry the pot and add in oil, celery, garlic, and onion.
Cook for 3 minutes.
Then, add the salt, pepper, and potatoes.
Add in the shrimp and tomatoes, and cook for 10 minutes.
Add the fish stock. Cook and bring the mixture to boil.
Break the fish into the mixture in chunks.
Serve and garnish with parsley.

Feta, Chili oil, and Thyme

Achlys Goddess loves to snack on this delicacy as she watches her chaotic superpower unfolds on humans!!

Preparation Time: 07 minutes
Cooking time: nil
Makes: 8
Ingredient list:

- 3 thyme sprigs
- 3 tarragon sprigs
- 8 oz cubed feta cheese
- 3 sliced birds eye peppers
- 3 tablespoons olive oil

Preparation:
Put the cheese in a clean jar.
Throw in the herbs and pepper.
Top with olive oil.
Store for 3 hours.

Poor Man's Caviar

Just ignore the name, this delicacy is rich, and you will love it!!!
Preparation Time: 08 minutes
Cooking time: nil
Makes: 1
Ingredient list:

- 2 tablespoons bread crumbs
- 2 handfuls green Greek olives (pitted)
- 2 peeled garlic cloves
- 2 handfuls black Greek olives (pitted)
- 8 tablespoons salted capers
- 1 large handful chopped parsley
- 2 tablespoons lemon juice

- 2 tablespoons olive oil
- 1 pinch black pepper
- 1 pinch Greek oregano

Preparation:

Wash the capers and olives under running water.

Allow draining for 3 minutes before patting dry with paper towels.

Blend the capers, garlic, olives, lemon juice, parsley, pepper, olive oil, bread crumbs, and oregano smoothly.

Serve with crackers.

Greek Mimosa

Mimosa made it to Greece!!

Preparation Time: 03 minutes
Cooking time: nil
Makes: 1
Ingredient list:

- 1-ounce sparkling Greek rose wine
- 2 tablespoons tsipouro
- 1 tablespoon lemon juice
- 1 tablespoon cinnamon syrup

Preparation:
Pour the tsipouro into a mixing glass.

Add the lemon juice and syrup.
Stir well.
Strain into your glass.
Top with champagne and rose wine.
Stir well.

Sex on the Greek!!

Oh my! The Greek version of Sex of the Beach is crazy!!!!

Preparation Time: 04 minutes
Cooking time: nil
Makes: 1
Ingredient list:

- 1 oz coconut cream
- 1 oz ouzo
- 1 oz Amaretto
- 1 squeeze lemon juice
- 3 oz orange juice

Preparation:

Toss in the Amaretto, ouzo, cream of coconut, and juices in a shaker of ice.
Shake well.
Sieve into a glass.
Add in ice cubes.
Garnish with an orange slice.

Ambrosia Drink

This cocktail is a perfect elixir, and this is why Athena gave Heracles this Ambrosia drink as a drink for immortality!!!

Preparation Time: 03 minutes
Cooking time: nil
Makes: 1
Ingredient list:

- 1 handful ice cubes
- 10ml Brut champagne
- 20ml Cognac
- 4ml lemon juice
- 20ml apple brandy
- 4ml Cointreau

Preparation:
Pour the ice cubes into a mixing glass.
Add the Cognac, apple brandy, lemon juice, and Cointreau.
Stir well.
Strain into your glass.
Top with the Brut.

Honey, Walnuts, and Yogurt

This combination of honey, walnuts, and yogurt is super delicious. Let's try it!

Preparation Time: 04 minutes
Cooking time: nil
Makes: 3
Ingredient list:

- 3 handfuls toasted walnuts (warm)
- 1 pinch cinnamon powder
- 8 tablespoons honey
- 1 pinch vanilla extract
- 24 tablespoons Greek yogurt (strained)

Preparation:

Blend the walnuts and honey till smooth.
Add the yogurt and vanilla to a bowl. Combine well.
Serve the yogurt in bowls.
Top with the walnut mixture.
Add a sprinkle of cinnamon.

Tzatziki

We can't talk about Greek legendary recipes without mentioning this delicious and creamy delicacy!!

Preparation Time: 07 minutes
Cooking time: nil
Makes: 1 cup
Ingredient list:

- 1 teaspoon salt
- 1 teaspoon pepper
- 1 minced garlic
- 8 tablespoons Greek yogurt
- 1 pinch lemon zest
- 1 grated, drained English cucumber
- 1 tablespoon chopped dill

Preparation:
Whisk the lemon juice, zest, cucumber, yogurt, garlic, and dill in a bowl. Chill and serve when ready.

Spicy Watermelon Salad

Having watermelon infused in your salad can sound odd, but with a dash of mint, cheese, and chili, you can have an extraordinary dose of awesomeness on a plate!!

Preparation Time: 08 minutes
Cooking time: nil
Makes: 2
Ingredient list:

- 2 cups cubed watermelon
- 2 tablespoons olive oil
- 30z crumbled feta cheese
- 1 handful lemon zest
- 1 sliced small red onion
- 1 diced chili (red)

- 1 teaspoon salt
- 1 teaspoon pepper
- 1 handful chopped mint leaves

Preparation:
Combine the lemon zest, olive oil, and chili in a bowl. Keep aside to allow marinating.
Place the watermelon pieces on a large plate.
Add a sprinkle of red onion, feta, and mint leaves.
Serve and garnish with a drizzle of the lemon zest oil.

Avgolemono

This meal will remind us of the Greek god, Agamemnon!!

Preparation Time: 10 minutes
Cooking time: 15 minutes
Makes: 2
Ingredient list:

- 1 medium egg yolk
- 1 handful chopped dill
- 1 teaspoon salt
- 1 teaspoon pepper
- 1 cup chicken broth
- 1 cup white rice (cooked)
- 1 pound chicken (shredded without bones)

- 3 tablespoons lemon juice

Preparation:
Combine the broth, pepper, and sauce in a pan.
Allow boiling for 4 minutes.
Scoop a part of the hot mixture in your food processor.
Toss in the egg yolk, 1 handful of rice, and lemon juice.
Process till smooth.
Transfer the processed mixture back into the pot with the remaining broth mixture.
Stir well.
Add the chicken and the remaining rice.
Cover and allow cooking for 10 minutes.
Throw in the dill.

Greek Mojito

Every country has its version of the mojito, and here is the Greek version of the cast spelling cocktail!! (Did you know that "mojito" means to cast a spell? We bet that you didn't!!)

Preparation Time: 04 minutes
Cooking time: nil
Makes: 1
Ingredient list:

- 1-ounce Metaxa
- 2 mint sprigs
- 1 dash lemon juice
- 1 dash lime juice
- 1 teaspoon brown sugar
- 1 oz club soda

Preparation:
Combine the Metaxa, mint, juices, sugar, and ice cubes into a shaker.
Strain into a glass.
Top with the soda.
Garnish with mint.

Greek Chocolate Mousse and Biscuits

Behold! This dish is the sweet delicacy that Zeus fed on as a kid!!

Preparation Time: 06 minutes
Cooking time: 07 minutes
Makes: 2
Ingredient list:

- 20ml warm milk
- 50g dark chocolate (couverture)
- 50g milk chocolate
- 4 crushed beurre
- 50g strained yogurt

Preparation:

Combine the two types of chocolate in a bowl.
Melt in a microwave saucer.
Pour the warm milk over the chocolate. Mix well.
Pour the mixture into a pan.
Stir over low heat.
Serve a part of the beurre in a glass.
Top with the yogurt.
Followed by the chocolate mousse.
And top with more beurre.

Greek Salad

This Greek version of a salad ought to win an award because this recipe is phenomenal!!

Preparation Time: 06 minutes
Cooking time: nil
Makes: 1
Ingredient list:

- 1 handful sliced red onion
- 5 pitted Kalamata olives
- 1 sliced cucumber (seedless)
- 1 tablespoon olive oil
- 1 pinch salt
- 1 pinch pepper
- 1 chunked vine tomato

- 1 dash red wine vinegar
- 1 handful dried oregano
- 30g crumbled feta

Preparation:
Combine the vinegar, salt, pepper, and oil in a bowl. Whisk well.
Arrange the sliced cucumber in a bowl. Add the onion, olives, and tomato.
Sprinkle the feta and oregano, and drizzle the vinegar dressing over it.

Greek Doctor

There is a doctor in Greece, yes, a cocktail!!!
Preparation Time: 03 minutes
Cooking time: nil
Makes: 1
Ingredient list:

- 1-part sour and sweet mix
- 1-ounce orange vodka
- 1-ounce orange juice
- 1-ounce peach vodka
- 1 dash ouzo

Preparation:

Add the ouzo, vodkas, and ouzo in a shaker of ice.
Shake well.
Strain into a glass.
Top with the sweet/sour mix and orange juice.
Stir well.

Galotyri

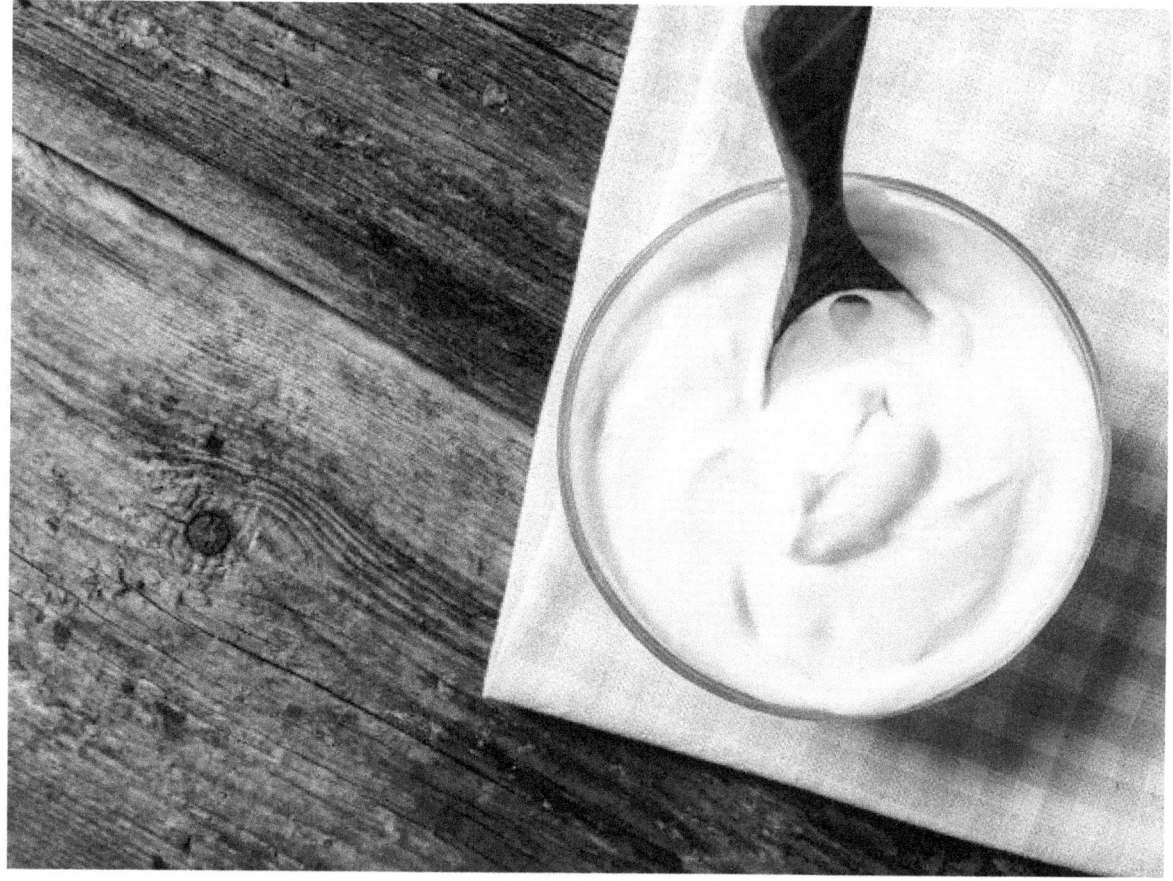

Have you thought of making cheese by yourself? This is an opportunity to learn how!!

Preparation Time: 15 minutes
Cooking time: nil
MAKES: 1 bowl
Ingredient list:

- 1 teaspoon salt
- 2 cups cow yogurt
- 20ml olive oil
- 100g sheep yogurt
- 70ml whole milk

Preparation:
Combine the cow yogurt and salt in a big bowl.
Whisk well.
Put the mixture in a cheesecloth and seal the ends of the cheesecloth.
Then you place the cheesecloth over the rim of a pot to drain excess water from the yogurt.
Place the pot and the cheesecloth in the refrigerator to chill for 24 hours and drain the liquid.
Transfer the cheese to a bowl, and add the milk, oil, and sheep yogurt.
Mix well.
Serve and garnish with pepper and thyme.

Chickpea Soup

Getting cold in Greece, try this awesome comfort soup!!

Preparation Time: 10 minutes
Cooking time: 45 minutes
Makes: 1
Ingredient list:

- 1 dash lemon juice
- 1 minced small onion
- 150g dried chickpeas (soaked)
- 40g olive oil
- 1 minced garlic clove
- 1 teaspoon dried oregano

Preparation:
Boil the soaked chickpeas in a pot of water.
Drain the chickpeas after 4 minutes.
Pour olive oil in a pot, and sauté the garlic and onion.
Throw in the chickpeas and 1 cup of water.
Cook till the chickpeas are tender (add more water if necessary).
Toss in pepper, olive oil, and salt.
Allow simmering for 10 minutes more.
Throw in the oregano and lemon juice.

Fasolatha

From generation to generation, this Greek delicacy has been there. Make way for this delicious Greek classic that was created by god Alon!!

Preparation Time: 10 minutes
Cooking time: 1 hour 15 minutes
Makes: 2
Ingredient list:

- 1 tablespoon pepper
- 1 tablespoon salt
- 1 cup water
- 1 sliced carrot
- 1 chopped celery stalk
- 1 sliced onion
- 1 pinch dried oregano

- 3 ounces diced tomatoes
- 1 pinch dried thyme
- 1 teaspoon tomato paste
- 1 teaspoon chopped parsley
- 2 tablespoons olive oil
- 2 handfuls soaked kidney beans (white)

Preparation:
Boil the soaked beans for 3 minutes.
Drain and discard the liquid.
Add 1 cup of water, celery, carrot, onion, olive oil, oregano, pepper, thyme, salt, tomato paste, and tomato.
Cover and cook for 1 hour.
Add the parsley when the beans are tender.

Conclusion

There you go!!

30 delicious and amazing recipes that Greek gods and goddesses enjoyed during their stay on earth.

The fact that these meals are meals that are associated with Greek gods/goddesses is not the only reason why we have decided to make a cookbook for them, it is the fact that although these meals are classical, they are still as relevant and delicious today just as they used to be back in the day!!!

These 30 recipes are recipes that you should start experimenting on immediately, so, go on, cook like a Greek god and goddess!!

Don't miss out!

Visit the website below and you can sign up to receive emails whenever Ida Smith publishes a new book. There's no charge and no obligation.

https://books2read.com/r/B-A-LRXL-UIIMB

BOOKS 2 READ

Connecting independent readers to independent writers.